UNDERSTANDING THE CHRONOLOGY OF
Revelation

Was Revelation Written in
Chronological Order?

Does a Reader Have a Right
to Rearrange this Great book?

Lyle E Cooper

WESTBOW
P R E S S®
A DIVISION OF THOMAS NELSON
& ZONDERVAN

WestBow Press books may be ordered through booksellers or by contacting:

WestBow Press
A Division of Thomas Nelson & Zondervan
1663 Liberty Drive
Bloomington, IN 47403
www.westbowpress.com
1 (866) 928-1240

Scripture taken from the King James Version of the Bible.

ISBN: 978-1-9736-9518-9 (sc)
ISBN: 978-1-9736-9517-2 (e)

Print information available on the last page.

WestBow Press rev. date: 7/2/2020

CONTENTS

INTRODUCTION

How God taught me about Revelation

My study of Revelation started with the Holy Spirit gently pushing me to begin to study Revelation and end times. His push got so powerful that for about three years I read nothing else but end-times passages in the bible. I read Daniel, Revelation, and the minor prophets on the end times, over and over; but mostly Revelation, while praying much in the Spirit. I probably read Daniel and Revelation over a hundred times. I did not try to use human understanding at that time to attempt to understand any of it. I was depositing it in my spirit and waiting on the Holy Spirit to teach. I told the Lord I would come with an "empty slate."

The Midpoint of the Week "Clearly Marked"

Finally, one day as I was reading Daniel 9: 27, when my eyes and my mind got to the word "midst," suddenly God spoke to me in what seemed like an audible voice:

"You could find that exact midpoint 'clearly marked' in the book of Revelation."

I was suddenly "in the Spirit," and could not speak, but my spirit man immediately spoke and ask "How would I find that?"

He answered, "Every time I mentioned an event that would begin at the midpoint and go to the end of the week, I always included the 3½ year period of time. When you find the mentions of the 3½ years, you will be very close to the exact midpoint."

Then, almost as an afterthought, he concluded: "In fact, you could find the entire 70th-week 'clearly marked.' "

When He said this, He also revealed to me without words the reason I could find the entire 70th-week would be that God would use the *same marker* to mark the beginning of the week, the midpoint of the week, and the end the week. That came as a download of information, not in words.

This event started me on a diligent search. I already knew about the five mentions of the 3½ years He spoke of: two given as 1260 days, two given as 42 months, and one given the way Daniel wrote, as "time, times and half of time." So I concentrated my search on chapters 11, 12, and 13 in Revelation.

I guess I studied these chapters hours each day for perhaps 2 months, trying to find the exact midpoint "clearly marked." During this time I often asked God, for help. I began to understand how John broke from his timeline of the seals, trumpets, and vials between the sixth and seventh seals, and the sixth and seventh trumpets as a kind of intermission. I began to ask God about that, too.

I came to realize John's narrative was like a long play with intermissions. I named his break between the sixth and seventh seals an intermission. At a play, when an intermission comes, the curtain is closed and they rearrange the setting for the next act. Then I understood what John did. You see, before Jesus opens the seventh seal to begin the 70th-week with God's wrath, the setting must be rearranged. Two events must take place before the seventh seal can be opened to start the 70th-week and begin the trumpet judgments: the two events are the sealing of the 144,000 and the church caught up to heaven before the 70th-week begins. Chapter 7 shows us these two events.

The church will be raptured before God's wrath begins, and it begins with the great earthquake at the sixth seal. John saw the raptured church in heaven in chapter 7, right after this great earthquake. This does not mean the rapture came after the earthquake, for they were already in heaven when John saw this great crowd, too large to number.

Before the seventh seal opens the 70th-week, the sealing of the 144,000 will be accomplished for their protection from the trumpet judgments. John left the real-time narrative of the breaking of the seals to "rearrange the setting" before he showed us the breaking of the seventh seal. The sealing of the 144,000 will be accomplished and the church will be in heaven, before Jesus opens the 7th seal to begin the 70th-week.

I wish to comment here on this crowd "too large to number." There will be only one group shown in Revelation that will be "too large to number." When the bride of Christ is caught up, it will be all those who have died in Christ for perhaps 50 generations. This alone will be a huge number, but added to this number will be all those who are alive and in Christ whom Jesus will snatch up. And added to that, all the children in the world under the age of accountability. Together, this crowd will be billions of people. This crowd John saw around the throne will be far bigger than any group from the 70th-week. In other words, when we read of a group of people too large to number, we can know it is the church, caught up to heaven. Just to compare, it would take a person nearly 32 years to count to a billion, counting one number a second.

I discovered the same kind of thing between the sixth and seventh trumpets. I called this intermission the midpoint intermission, for it is near the midpoint of the week. Now I see the midpoint intermission only as chapter 10 and chapter 14. I cannot include chapters 11, 12, or 13 as part of an intermission. There are five mentions of the last 3½ years in these chapters.

As I was studying chapter 11, trying to find the "exact midpoint, clearly marked"—as Jesus said I could— I suddenly saw something that did not quite fit. John is in his midpoint intermission, so I thought then, telling us about the city that will be trampled, and the coming of the two witnesses, when John abruptly tells us that the second woe is past, the third comes quickly and then sounds the seventh trumpet—right in the intermission. In other words, a real-time event during or inside an intermission.

As an example, suppose you are watching the nutcracker, and just before the king mouse is about to kill the nutcracker, the curtains close and an announcer tells the crowd it is intermission time and encourages all to go and get refreshments. Since there are many people there, it takes you a while to get to the end of your aisle. Suddenly, when most of the people are out of the seating area, you see the curtain re-open, see the girl throw her slipper and hit the king mouse in the head, and see the nutcracker win the battle. Then, just as suddenly, the curtain closes again. The most exciting part of the play happened during the intermission.

Of course this would never happen, but it seemed at the time that is what John did. He wrote of a real-time event in the middle of an intermission. Suddenly I realized that the exact midpoint was "marked" by the seventh trumpet. This is what suddenly came to me. I flipped quickly to the seventh vial and read "It is done." Several translations of this verse (Rev. 16:17) use the word "finished."

Then I knew I had found what He sent me to find: the midpoint "clearly marked." I rushed back to the seventh seal and read of the 30 minutes of silence. Then I knew I had found the entire 70th-week "clearly marked," exactly as Jesus had said. What better way to begin the 70th-week of Daniel than with 30 minutes of silence?

After the fact, I found an even easier way to show where the midpoint is. Jesus told those in Judea to flee, the moment they see the abomination. We can prove it will be the abomination that will divide the week into two halves from Daniel 9:27 and 2 Thessalonians 2. When anyone other than the high priest enters the holy of holies in the temple, the daily sacrifices must end: the temple will be desecrated and will have to be cleansed before any more animals can be sacrificed.

This is what happened when Antiochus Epiphanes stopped the daily sacrifices when he slaughtered a pig in the temple, and place an image of Zeus in the Most Holy place in the temple. It was 2300 days later before Zerubbabel's temple could be cleansed and the sacrifices continued. Therefore, when Daniel wrote "he shall cause the sacrifice and the oblation to cease," it is the very event that will divide the 70th-week.

We find that fleeing of those living in Judea, just as Jesus had told them, in Revelation 12:6. Therefore we know the abomination event will be one or two seconds before verse 12:6 where they begin fleeing. (We should include a second or two for response time.) If we back up verse by verse to find the abomination, we won't find it. John did not see it and did not record it. But if we back up verse by verse looking for a marker, we will find the seventh trumpet. The seventh trumpet will sound in heaven to "mark" the time on earth that the man of sin enters the temple and declares that he is God.

When the man of sin enters the Holy of Holies, the temple will immediately be declared polluted and unfit for sacrifices, and the daily sacrifices must then cease—Just what Daniel 9:27 states. In other words, it will be the man of sin that stops the daily sacrifices, according to Paul in 2 Thessalonians 2.

CHAPTER 1

The Vision of the Throne Room

After I discovered that God marked the entire 70th-week with 7's, leaving the first 6 seals *out* of the 70th-week, I went back to chapters 4 & 5 to study them in-depth. I knew God would leave clues showing us that these seals were not in the 70th-week. In chapter 4, John saw a vision of the throne room. Some might imagine John was seeing the throne room without a vision, but this is not so: most of Revelation is one long vision, and the throne room was a part of John's vision.

He saw the throne of God and someone on the throne, he saw the four beasts with many eyes, he saw the 24 elders around the throne, and he saw the Holy Spirit as seven lamps of fire or the Seven Spirits of God there in the throne room.

I asked the Father to show me in these chapters proof that the first seals were NOT in the 70th-week. I studied these chapters for a few weeks, and finally got stuck on John weeping much. (It was the Holy Spirit, not me.) I could not seem to get away from that. I asked God why we needed to know that John wept, and why much?

Finally He spoke and said only "It shows timing."

I heard His voice again, but this time thought it was in my spirit, and probably not an "audible voice" others would have heard. I studied these chapters another few weeks, and could not find "timing" anywhere, so I was often asking God for help. Finally He spoke again and said, "it also shows the movement of time."

I studied diligently, but I could not find any "movement of time" anywhere. Finally, God had mercy on me and spoke again:

"I will ask you three questions. Until you can answer them correctly you will never understand this part of John's vision."

Then He asked me three questions from chapters 4 & 5.

Three Questions on Revelation chapters 4 and 5

This won't be exactly word for word, for it has been a few years now, but it will be close.

1. "Why did John not immediately see Me at the right hand of the Father in chapter four? I ascended back into heaven years before John saw this vision. There are over a dozen verses showing that I went to be at the right hand of the Father. Why then did John not immediately see Me at the right hand of the Father?"

As before, when He spoke, I was "in the spirit" and could not answer by thinking of an answer and speaking. However, my spirit man answered, "I cannot answer that question."

Again He spoke.

2. "John watched a search to find one worthy to open the seals—a search that ended in failure—and that is the reason John wept much: no man was found worthy. However, if you read ahead, you find that I was found

worthy to break the seals. Why then was I not found in that first search?"

Again my spirit man answered, "Lord, I cannot answer that." Then He asked me the third question:

3. "If you notice in chapter 4, the Holy Spirit was still in the throne room. I told the disciples that as soon as I ascended, I would send Him down. Why was the Holy Spirit still in the throne room in chapter 4?"

Again my spirit man said that he could not answer this question. The Lord did not say more at that time. I studied diligently on that vision of the throne room, trying to answer His questions. I could not see any timing. I could not see the movement of time. I could not figure out why Jesus was not at the right hand of the Father. I could not figure out why "no man was found." I could not figure out why the Holy Spirit was still there. I spent weeks looking and asking God for help.

Finally after three or four more weeks of study, I heard His voice again. He said, "go and study chapter 12."

I did not want to do this. I was in an intense study of chapters 4 & 5, and the last thing I wanted to do was to go to another chapter. However, I was obedient and flipped the pages of my bible to chapter 12. When I got my bible opened to chapter 12, He spoke again.

"Chapter 12 was Me introducing John to the Dragon, and in particular what the Dragon would be doing in the last half of the week. Count how many times the Dragon is mentioned, including pronouns."

So I counted, carefully: 32 times. I replied, "I see that this chapter is about the dragon. I counted 32 times." I was not "in the spirit" at this time, because I marked all the mentions of the Dragon and then counted them up. He waited for me.

He spoke again.

"I also chose to show John how the dragon attempted to kill me as a young child. Those first five verses were a 'history lesson' for John."

He let that sink in, and after a minute or two He said,

"Now you can go back to chapters 4 & 5."

I flipped back to the vision of the throne room, and in just a few minutes had the answer to all three questions. The key I needed was "history lesson." I suddenly realized that John was looking, in the vision, into the throne room of the past, at a time just before Jesus rose from the dead.

Most people never notice that Jesus Christ, the Son of God, was not seen at the right hand of the Father; John saw only the Father on the throne. Many verses tell us Jesus went to sit at the right hand of the Father, so we would expect John to have seen both the Father and the Son when he saw the vision of the throne room. Stephen saw Him there. We must remember, John was seeing a vision of the throne room, not the throne room of 95 CE. John did not see Jesus the Son at the right hand of the father, for, at that time in the vision, He was still on the earth or under the earth. From eternities past to eternities future, there has only been one small amount of time where Jesus was not at the right hand of the Father, and that was during the 32 years or so that He was on earth.

When John wrote, "no man was found worthy" to take the book and open the seals, that tells us that Jesus had not yet risen from the dead. He was not worthy to take the book until after He had risen from the dead and became "the redeemer." Finally, the Holy Spirit was still in the throne room because Jesus had not yet ascended to send Him down.

Then, as we read further into chapter 5, we see that another search started as soon as the first search failed to find anyone worthy. Some people argue that John did not call it a "search." In my mind, if someone is "found," then someone was looking or searching.

God sent this angel on a mission; to find someone worthy to open the book. Since John mentioned that this took place in heaven, on earth, and then under the earth, I think the term "search" fits what John wrote.

John wept much because no man was found in this first search he had watched. Make no mistake here: this angel was searching for one worthy to open the seals so the book could be opened—and John watched that first search take place; first in heaven, then on earth and then under the earth. That first search failed to find someone worthy, and John wrote, "no man was found." If no one was "found" then someone was trying to "find" one worthy to open the seals and open the book—so we know this angel was searching.

We don't know how long John wept, but it could have been hours or days. Reading on, we see that finally someone came up to John and told him he could stop weeping, for someone had been found worthy: "the Lion of the tribe of Judah, the Root of David, hath *prevailed* to open the book, and to loose the seven seals thereof."

Here we see the passing of time. The first search ended in failure, and John wept much, but it seems this angel started another search as soon as the first search ended. This hints that perhaps this search for one worthy to take this book and open the seals had been ongoing for some time; another search starting the moment the first one failed to find anyone worthy.

What did Jesus "prevail" over, to become worthy? He prevailed over death. He conquered death by rising from the dead. When He rose, He became the redeemer of the human race. If He had failed to conquer death, according to Paul, and rise from the dead, we would still be in our sins. Before Christ rose from the dead, "no man was found worthy," including Jesus. But after He rose from the dead, He was immediately found worthy. It seems that only someone who conquered death could be worthy to open the seals.

Someone came up to John and told him to stop weeping, for someone had prevailed to take the book and open the seals. Then John turned and saw a Lamb, "having been slain." That Lamb was simply not there the moment before. John got to see in the vision, the moment Jesus ascended, after telling Mary not to touch Him, for He had not yet ascended. Once Mary left Him, He ascended and entered the throne room, and John got to see His arrival into the throne room, in the vision. We read that He came with the Holy Spirit, who was then immediately sent down to the earth.

> 6. And I beheld, and, lo, in the midst of the throne and of the four beasts, and in the midst of the elders, stood a Lamb as it had been slain, having seven horns and seven eyes, *which are the seven Spirits of God sent forth into all the earth.* (King James Version, Revelation 5) (Emphasis added)

Some people want to argue that Jesus was there all the time, but just not seen. Sorry, but this was a vision given by God to make a point: to set the timing of the first seal. John saw exactly what God wanted him to see, and John wrote exactly what he saw: a throne room where Jesus was not seen at the right hand of the Father and a search for one worthy that ended up failing to find someone worthy. Both these things point to a time before Jesus rose from the dead. That Jesus was there but just not seen is a weak argument: the main them of the entire book is the revealing of the Son. To imagine He was there but just not seen does not fit with the rest of scripture.

God had a problem: He wanted to introduce John to the "book" or scroll with seven seals, but He also wanted to begin while the book was still in the hand of the Father, which was before Jesus ascended. To accomplish this, God would have to show John something from the past—in other words, things that would be history to John. It was perhaps 95 AD when John saw this vision. How could God show John and future readers that this part of the vision was history in 95 AD and not something in John's future?

God chose to show a throne room with Jesus absent, the Holy Spirit still in the throne room, and then a search for one worthy that failed to find someone. People have disagreed with me more, over these two chapters than any other place in Revelation. Some imagine Jesus was there but just not seen.

Some imagine He just suddenly became visible in chapter 5. I think it is clear: God chose words carefully to show Jesus not seen, not found worthy, and then later found worthy and then seen—to show us timing and the passing of time. Remember, the first two things Jesus spoke to me was that this passage shows "timing" and "the movement of time."

This vision of the throne room sets the context for the seals. When did Jesus ascend? Somewhere around 32 AD. The moment after Jesus entered the throne room, the first thing He did was get the scroll from the right hand of the Father and begin opening the seals.

7. And he came and took the book out of the right hand of him that sat upon the throne. (King James Version, Revelation 5)

No one can find 2000 years between any of these verses, because it is not there. The Holy Spirit intended to show that Jesus opened the first seals about 32 AD.

The first seal then, the rider on the white horse, will be something within the timeframe of around 32 AD. The white horse and rider are to represent the church sent out with the gospel to make disciples of all nations. John used the color white 17 times in Revelation and every other time to represent righteousness. Of course the white color of the horse must also represent righteousness. It would be ludicrous to think otherwise. The horse is to represent warfare. The bow without arrows may represent spiritual warfare.

The second seal, with the red horse and rider, the third seal with the black horse and rider, and the fourth seal with the pale horse and rider are to represent the Dragon's or Satan's attempts to stop the gospel from advancing; using war, famine, pestilences and wild beasts. These riders ride together but God limited their theater of operation to one-fourth of the earth. Of course that one-fourth would be centered on Jerusalem, where the Gospel began.

That would probably include Europe, the Middle East, and Africa. Where have all the famines in our lifetime been? Most have been in Africa. That was the black horse and rider at work. Where did the black plague hit—twice—killing nearly one-third of the population each time? In Europe. That was the pale horse and rider at work: "Death." Where did two world wars begin? Again in Europe. That was the red horse and rider at work. Without much doubt, the third world war will begin in this same quarter of the earth.

John wrote, "power was given unto them..." (Revelation 6:8). I began to ask God about that: "God, who is 'them?'"

He answered, "it is right there in the verse: read it again."

I asked Him several times because I could not find it in that verse. He answered the same thing every time. It took me a while to find it. He wrote that "power was given unto "them" to kill with the sword:" the red horse rider was given a great sword. "Power was given unto "them" to kill with hunger:" the black horse was to bring famine or hunger. "Power was given unto "them" to kill with death:" the pale horse rider's title was "Death." So I understood that these three ride together, while the rider on the white horse rides alone. Of course these three riders failed to stop the church, for today the gospel is almost everywhere on the planet. These horses and riders are probably symbolic.

Next I noticed that at the fifth seal was the first hint of a long time of waiting. This time of waiting is the church age. I wondered about the answer given to those under the altar at the fifth seal. They were told to wait for a season until the rest of the martyrs "should be killed as they were." All those martyrs were not killed the same way; some were fed to lions, some were crucified, and some were beheaded. "Killed as they were" does not mean how each martyr was killed, for there were different ways the martyrs were put to death.

Finally I understood it: Those under the altar had to wait for the last martyr to be killed as they were killed: as church age martyrs. God is waiting for the completed number.

11. And white robes were given unto every one of them; and it was said unto them, that they

should rest yet for a little season, until their fellow servants also and their brethren, *that should be killed as they were, should be fulfilled.* (King James Version, Revelation 6) (Emphasis added.)

The ESV puts it: "*until the number* of their fellow servants and their brothers should be complete." (Revelation 6:11 ESV)

The NASB puts it: "*until the number* of their fellow servants and their brethren who were to be killed even as they had been, would be completed also." (Revelation 6:11 NASB)

Douay-Rheims puts it: "till their fellow servants and their brethren, who are to be slain even as they, *should be filled up.*" (Revelation 6:11 Douay- Rheims)

Weymouth puts it: "*until the full number* of their fellow bondservants should also complete—namely of their brethren who were soon to be killed just as they had been." (Revelation 6:11 Weymouth)

The Emphasized Bible puts it: "*until the number should be made full* of their fellow-servants also, and their brethren, who were about to be slain as even, they." (Revelation 6:11 Emphasized Bible)(Emphasis added to the above quotes)

It seems then, that God has a number in mind: the entire number of martyrs of the church age. They must wait for this completed number before judgment will come. John was not told this completed number, but we don't need to know it. What we do know is, the rapture of the church will end the church age, and any martyrs killed after the rapture will not be "church age martyrs" as these are, but will be "Day of the Lord" or "70th-week" martyrs: a different group with a different number.

In other words, these martyrs of the church age will have to wait for the rapture of the church that will end the church age.

John gave us another strong hint of a pre-tribulation rapture. What is the next event John mentions? It is the sixth seal. At the sixth seal, John wrote, "the day of His wrath has come." The sixth seal then is the start of God's wrath on the earth.

We know that God will catch us up before He pours out His wrath. At least, we should know it. Paul tells us this in 1 Thessalonians 5: the rapture will come just before wrath and just before the Day of the Lord or the Day of Wrath. Therefore the rapture must come before the sixth seal but after the fifth seal. I believe that the rapture will come one moment before the sixth seal earthquake. This great earthquake at the 6th seal will be Paul's sudden destruction that comes a moment after the rapture. This is just one more proof that John wrote with a strict chronology. Paul tells us that we are not to go through God's wrath.

> 10. And to wait for his Son from heaven, whom he raised from the dead, even Jesus, which delivered us from the wrath to come. (King James Version, 1 Thessalonians 1)

> 9. *For God hath not appointed us to wrath*, but to obtain salvation by our Lord Jesus Christ (King James Version, 1 Thessalonians 5)

In Paul's classic rapture passage—where Jesus will raise the dead in Christ first, then will catch up those who are "in Christ" and alive on earth—he does not change subjects in chapter 5 but gives us timing information for the rapture. In short, a suddenly is coming: at a time when people are saying "peace and safety." (A time like today.) The sudden event will be the dead in Christ rising. Then, instantly after that, Jesus will catch up and change those who are alive and in Christ, and together, all will rise to meet Christ in the air. However, at that same time, those living in darkness will get the "sudden destruction" and cannot escape.

In chapter 5, Paul wrote that those living in the light of the Gospel get "salvation" or get raptured, and get to "live together with Him." In chapter 4 he put it: "so shall we ever be with the Lord." We will get to "live together with Him," or be with Him, by way of the rapture or being caught up. Here Paul is telling us when: it will be a moment before the Day of His wrath begins. We get raptured, but those living in darkness get left behind and get "sudden destruction" which is the beginning of the "Day of His wrath."

Many readers don't understand Paul here: that at the same time those living "in Christ" are raptured, those left behind face the "sudden destruction." A moment after the dead in Christ rise, Paul's sudden destruction hits: which will be a worldwide earthquake caused by the dead in Christ rising. Many of the dead in Christ have been dead for centuries, and their bodies turned back to dust, as the bible puts it. But in one instant of time, God will bring that dust together—whether at the atom level or the quark level or even smaller particles—we don't know. However, it seems from Matthew 27, where Jesus raised the elders of the Old Testament saints and there was a great earthquake, that when the dead in Christ rise, there will also be an earthquake. Since those "in Christ" will be found around the world, it will be a worldwide earthquake. Remember, when Jesus died, it is written, "the earth did quake...and the graves were opened..." (Matthew 27:51-52)

This gives us a hint that when God raises the dead, that raising will cause an earthquake. I believe at that time when Jesus died and then rose again, He resurrected the elders of the Old Testament. Adam would surely have been one of them.

Abraham another. The atoms that made up their bodies could have been scattered for hundreds of miles, or thousands of miles. Adam died before the flood, and the flood rearranged everything. The particles that used to make up Adam's body could have been separated by thousands of miles by time and by the flood. In one moment of time God brought together the particles that used to make up the bodies of those dead saints, and that caused the great shaking as recorded in Matthew 27. I believe He brought their bodies together when Jesus died, causing the earthquake, then brought them to life when Jesus rose. They could not get resurrection bodies until after Jesus' resurrection.

> 51. And, behold, the veil of the temple was rent in twain from the top to the bottom; and the earth did quake, and the rocks rent;
>
> 52. And the graves were opened, and many bodies of the saints which slept arose,
>
> 53. And came out of the graves after his resurrection, and went into the holy city, and appeared unto many. (King James Version, Matthew 27)

John tells us there will also be an earthquake when God raises the two witnesses. It will be the same with the church—those who have died in Christ: many have been dead for centuries and their atoms scattered far from the burial site. When the dead in Christ rise, it will cause a worldwide earthquake: an earthquake just as we see at the sixth seal.

Some people have doubts about this, but God will certainly re-create the bodies of the Saints who have passed. It will be their body, put back together, and then raised. But at the moment of raising, the Holy Spirit will change the old body into a resurrection body.

It is no mistake that John saw the raptured church in heaven shortly after that, in Revelation chapter 7. Many have failed to recognize this group, too large to number, as the "just raptured" church because someone in the vision told John they "come out of great tribulation." Immediately most people think of the days of great tribulation that Jesus spoke of.

However, there is a big problem with that theory. John has not yet even started the 70th-week, much less arrived at the midpoint and the time the Beast would be revealed. The days of great tribulation that Jesus spoke of would come after the midpoint. They will not begin until the false prophet shows up and the image and mark are created. This does not come in Revelation until after chapter 14. It is not until chapter 15 that we see the beheaded arriving in heaven from "those days" of "great tribulation" that Jesus spoke of. (Quotes from Matthew 24.) Therefore it seems that John is not talking about the days of great tribulation that Jesus talked about.

Others say this large group cannot be the raptured church, because the Greek verb tense of "come out of great tribulation," is that they come out "one by one." In other words, "these are they which [one by one] came out of great tribulation." The rapture, on the other hand, is a one time, sudden event, so some people insist that this group could not be the raptured saints. I disagree. The vast majority of those caught up in the rapture will be the dead in Christ. Since generation after generation of believers—over almost 2000 years—will be a far greater number than those who are alive and remain on earth: just one generation. John is not telling us here how they got to heaven, but how they came into Christ that allowed them to be caught up in the rapture.

How did the dead in Christ come "into" Christ: that is, how did they pass from death to life? Of course, they came one by one, as each heard the gospel and believed. At the moment they believed and confessed, and were born again, they changed from eternal death to eternal life. Could the Author's intent of this scripture be that when one is born again, they come out of the great tribulation that is life on earth as a sinner? I believe the answer is yes.

Ellicott's Commentary has this to say;

"They are those who come, not all at once, but gradually. The saints of God are continually passing into the unseen world, and taking their place among the spirits of just men made perfect."

In the Greek, it is "they washed" their robes, meaning, while they were alive on the earth. Each believer washes their robes when they are born again. Again it seems to portray life on earth as a believer, not the sudden transport into heaven. These believers' robes were not made white by the rapture. Neither was their robes made white by their suffering. They were made white while alive on the earth, by believing in the blood of Jesus Christ.

Gill's Commentary has this to say:

"the great tribulation, out of which they came, is not to be restrained to any particular time of trouble, but includes all that has been, is, or shall be..."

The Pulpit Commentary puts it this way:

> "The question arises What is 'the great tribulation' referred to? Probably all the tribulation which has been passed through by the redeemed, all that which pertained to the life through which they have passed."

Alford's Commentary said it this way:

> "I would rather understand it of the whole sum of the trials of the saints of God, viewed by the Elder as now complete, and designated by this emphatic and general name..."

Benson's commentary says,

> "Yet these could not be all martyrs, for the martyrs could not be such a multitude as no *man could number...* All these may be said, more or less, to come *out of great tribulation,* of various kinds, wisely and graciously allotted by God to all his children..." (Emphasis added)

I agree with these commentaries. Of course others believe John has no real chronology, and chapter seven is showing us a picture of those who died during "those days" of "great tribulation" that Jesus spoke of. I can find no evidence elsewhere in Revelation that John writes against a strict chronology. It seems he is precise in his chronology throughout the book, except for his use of parentheses. Therefore I find it illogical that in this one instance he chose to show a picture of a future event.

What then was John talking about? He is talking about all the combined tribulations that the saints have gone through; some martyred, but all hated because Jesus was hated, during the entire church age.

Finally, of all the groups in Revelation, no group will come close to the number of those caught up at the rapture—perhaps 50 generations of believers. It is going to be a huge number, in the billions: far too many for a human to count. It will also be a far greater number that those who turn to Christ during the seven years.

For these reasons, I believe this great crowd must be the church: raptured a moment before the sixth seal earthquake. John did not see the rapture, so he did not record it, but he then saw the raptured church in heaven.

Chapter 7 is an intermission between the sixth and seventh seal. It is God rearranging the setting, because wrath is coming, and God wants 144,000 of Israel sealed for their protection, and wants the church pulled out to safety before the seventh seal officially opens the 70th-week of Daniel. The entire 70th-week will be God's wrath poured out in the trumpets and vials.

CHAPTER 2

Points to Ponder in considering John's Chronology

Since the last book in the bible is "the Revelation of Jesus Christ," one would expect it to be a revealing, not hiding or masking, and we will approach the book from this perspective. By this I mean, anything that makes good sense in its literal sense will certainly be taken as literal. Things that do not make good sense taken literally will then be taken as symbolic.

The main points of the book are the seven churches, the book sealed with seven seals—including what is written inside the book—the seven trumpets and the seven vials. The word "seven" is included in Revelation 36 times.

John wrote this amazing book with several series of numbered seven's. There are the seven churches, the seven seals, the seven trumpets, and finally the seven vials or bowls, filled with God's wrath, that will be poured out with associated plagues. John numbered the seven seals, the seven trumpets and the seven vials for their proper sequence. The 7 seals, the 7 trumpets, and the 7 vials form the timeline of the book. Many people feel the need to rearrange John's timeline to fit their theories, but they are mistaken. John wrote in chronological order. There is no need to rearrange.

There are also three woes, which are the last three trumpet judgments; also numbered for sequencing. John used timing phrases such as "after these things" or "after this," at least six times to transition from one part of the vision to another. These are also timing phrases.

Then there are verses like this: (Rev 8:1–2) "And when he had opened the seventh seal, there was silence in heaven about the space of half an hour. And I saw the seven angels which stood before God, and to them were given seven trumpets."

This shows us that all seven of the seals must be opened before the seven trumpets, in the exact order that John wrote it. In other words, no trumpet can sound until Jesus has opened all seven seals. This makes perfect sense because the seals are keeping the book closed. Once Jesus has opened the seals, then the book can be opened, so each trumpet judgment comes from what is written inside the book.

When John first saw the book, he emphasized how important this book is by weeping much when no man was found worthy to open the seals. It is to be understood that the seals are only there to prevent any unauthorized person from opening the book. In other words, it is the book that is the most important, not the seals. Some imagine that the seals are all there is to the book. That is not at all the intent of the Author. John wrote that the book was written "within." There is writing inside the book. We must understand that once the seals are opened, then the book is opened, and it is what is written inside the book that will finally cause the kingdoms of the world to be given back to Jesus and Satan removed from his position as "god of this world." It should be understood then that what we read after the 7th seal is opened is what is written inside the book.

I wonder why anyone would imagine that God, who was giving John this vision, would show things out of proper sequence when John numbered so many events for proper sequencing. However, many people feel the need to rearrange John's book to fit their theories. Some even imagine they can rearrange the numbered events. My axiom on Revelation is this:

> Any theory that must rearrange John's God-given chronology is immediately suspect and will be proven wrong.

In other words, in this vision, God showed these events to John in the order that they will come to pass and John wrote them in that same order. However, what is a writer to do, when several things happen at the same time? John could not write of five events going on at the same time, except by writing them one by one.

In chapters 11 through 13, God introduced John to five separate events that will begin near the midpoint and count down to the end of the week, so from chapter 13 to chapter 16, where the 70th-week comes to an end, there are five parallel paths to the end. Then John adds to those five, his narrative of the vision he saw. All five parallel countdowns are not written out as time progresses through the chapters. John only wrote of the starting points; but the numbers are counting down while John tells us what else he is seeing in the vision. It seems God did not show John the endpoint of these countdowns, except for the Two Witnesses, and the two Beasts. Each countdown will start on a different day, except perhaps the 42 months of the trampling of the city and the 1260 days of testifying by the Two Witnesses. It seems very likely that these two countdowns will begin on the same day.

Also the 1260 days of fleeing and the 3½ years of protection in chapter 12 may well start on the same day. John recorded these events in the same order God showed them to him. It seems likely that they will not all end on the same day since they will not all start on the same day.

When studying Revelation, we must keep in mind that the idea of parentheses was known in Greek writing, but they did not use any punctuation marks to show parentheses. We must discover parentheses by study alone.

> 1. The Revelation of Jesus Christ, which God gave unto him, to shew unto his servants things which must shortly come to pass; and he sent and signified it by his angel unto his servant John: (King James Version, Revelation 1)

Notice that in general, God showed John things that will "shortly" come to pass. Some people get hung up on this word "shortly" and imagine that for the most part, the book of Revelation took place in A.D. 70. They fail to recognize that "shortly" may well mean something different to God than to us.

> 10. I was in the Spirit on the Lord's day, and heard behind me a great voice, as of a trumpet. (King James Version, Revelation 1)

Some people seem to imagine that John was not only transported into heaven but transported into the future "Day of the Lord." This is not at all the intention of this verse. The messages to the churches, John being called up to heaven and the first five seals are before the Day of the Lord. John was speaking of Sunday, the day that our Lord rose from the dead, as "the Lord's day." There is scriptural evidence in the New Testament that the early church began coming together for meetings on Sunday.

> 7. And upon the first day of the week, when the disciples came together to break bread, Paul preached unto them, ready to depart on the morrow; and continued his speech until midnight. (King James Version, Acts 20)

Continuing in Revelation:

> 19. Write the things which thou *hast seen*, and the things which *are*, and the things which shall be *hereafter*; (King James Version, Revelation 1)

God told John to write things he had seen, things that were in his time, and things in his future—that is, future to him in perhaps 95 A.D. Therefore we must study to see which of these three periods of time John is writing about in any verse. It could be history, present, or future to John's time. A vision can show events of the past, events of the present, or events of the future; or all three combined.

> 1. After this I looked, and, behold, a door was opened in heaven: and the first voice which I heard was as it were of a trumpet talking with me; which said, Come up hither, and I will shew thee things which must be hereafter. (King James Version, Revelation 4)

Some people read this phrase, "after this" and imagine that John's meaning is "after the church age." There is no justification for this. John uses this phrase or a similar one to transition from one part of the vision to another six different times when God changed the subject in the vision. To imagine another meaning not really stated is stretching the scripture. If we read a little more, we see that it was *John* caught up to heaven (not the church), while he was still alive. Therefore to imagine this is after the church age is simply not good exegesis. This is about John being caught up—perhaps around 95 AD—so he could see these things and write this amazing book. In truth, in Revelation 4:1, John has not yet seen things in his vision that will "shortly come to pass." The first thing John saw was a vision of the throne room—but it was the throne room of his past.

Notice the phrase at the end of verse 4:1: "Come up hither, and I will shew thee things which must be hereafter."

This is a simple statement of fact, but many do not read it correctly. Notice carefully that if God chose to show John two or three events in the future (things hereafter), and finished the book with recipes of how to cook manna, He would not have gone against this verse. In other words, this verse does NOT say,

"I will shew thee "only" things which must be hereafter."

Yet many people read it that way. (I am not adding to Revelation.) They imagine that from this point on everything must be future. I can say it another way: God was free to show John some events in John's history if He chose to. The truth is, God did choose to show John things in his history.

CHAPTER 3

The Seals

John numbered each seal. Some people seem to think these numbers were added by translators, or that John was just keeping things straight in his mind. Some think that the numbers were only for the sequence that God showed the visions to John, but may not be the order in which they will happen. This is all human imagination. The Holy Spirit numbered them Himself because this is the order these events will happen. No one has any right to rearrange John's numbered events. If they do, their theory will be proven wrong.

We must understand that the seals are sealing a book, preventing this book from being opened except by a certain man. There is far more to this book that just the seals that are sealing it. Notice what John wrote about this book.

> 1. And I saw in the right hand of him that sat on the throne a book *written within* and on the backside, sealed with seven seals. (King James Version, Revelation 5)

The book is more than just seals: there are things written inside the book.

Notice this this book has writing inside or "within." Most people ignore this and imagine the seals are the entire book, and when John gets the 7th seal opened, the book is then finished. John did not write of the book being opened, but we must understand that what John wrote after Jesus opened the 7th seal must be what was written inside the book. In other words, the first trumpet judgment was the first event written inside the book.

My point is, no one can open this book, until first, Jesus has opened every seal. Often I read something like; "the seventh trumpet is sounded at the seventh seal." Such things are simply impossible. Until Jesus opens all seven of the seals, the book cannot be opened to begin the trumpet judgments. Finally, in chapter 8, Jesus opens the seventh seal and what we read from then on in Revelation, maybe to at least chapter 16, is written inside the book. The trumpet judgments, for example, are inside the book. No angel can sound a trumpet until Jesus has opened all seven seals so the book can be opened. John does not tell us, but I suspect that the entire 70th-week is written inside the book.

To imagine that after Jesus opens the 7 seals, there is no book to be opened, seems to ignore that in John's time, seals were used to prevent anyone from opening a document until whoever sealed it is present to open the seal or seals. However, some people still believe that the seals are all there is to this book. There must be a book to read once Jesus has opened all the seals, for John wrote that the book had writing "within."

Many people get zeroed in examining one tree (so to speak), when they need to back up so they can see the entire forest. What do I mean? How much of the book of Revelation is about this book sealed by seven seals? Chapters 4 & 5 are the context for the seals, so they must be included. Then chapter 6 through chapter 8 is John opening the seals. Then chapters 8 through 16 are, without much doubt, what is written inside the book. We can't be dogmatic, because John does not say this word for word, but only hints of it. I think that the entire 70th-week is what is written inside the book sealed with 7 seals. I think the text has hints of this. It makes good sense in my mind that the book contains the entire 70th-week. It is only a guess.

Therefore, we see that the chapters involved with this "book with seven seals" are chapters 4 through 16. That is 13 chapters out of 22 that are written about this book sealed with seven seals. How could anyone get a good understanding of the book of Revelation while ignoring this book with seven seals and what is written inside the book? This is one big area where people form incorrect theories on Revelation. Here are some things one should consider when thinking about this book sealed with 7 seals.

Any theory of Revelation should include the understanding that "the book" in Revelation 5 is a legal document created in heaven and sealed up with seven seals. We should consider the following points:

1. Neither God nor Satan could begin anything written on or about a seal before Jesus opened (or will open) that seal.

2. The purpose of the seals was to prevent anyone from opening the book, and beginning the events written in the book, until some man was found worthy to take the book and open the seals.

3. For the first four seals at least, once Jesus opened that seal, then what was written about that seal could legally begin, but not before. As examples, Jesus could not send out the church with the gospel until He opened that first

seal. Satan could not send out that red horse and rider until Jesus opened the second seal.

4. John numbered the seals for their proper order. Any theory that attempts to rearrange what John has numbered for sequencing will be proven wrong.

5. Nothing written in Revelation after the seventh seal can come to pass before Jesus opens all the seals so that He can then open the book. Therefore, any theory that moves a seal to align with a trumpet or a vial will be proven wrong. Any theory that must move a trumpet or vial to happen with a seal will be proven wrong. What we read in Revelation after the seventh seal is opened is what is written inside the book. For example, the trumpet judgments are written inside the book.

6. Neither God nor Satan could legally take the book and open the seals. It could only be opened by a man from the human race. Further, it would have to be a man who could redeem mankind—a man who could prevail over death and rise again—a man who could escape from Hades: the place of departed spirits.

7. There was a time when Jesus Christ was not found worthy to take the book and open the seals. John is clear on this: it is why he wept much. Jesus became worthy once He became the Redeemer, and one of those requirements was to prevail over death by rising from the dead.

God's goal is to get to the 7th trumpet, so Satan can be dethroned and the Kingdoms of this world be given back to Jesus. This is the great mystery in Revelation 10. I suspect it was Satan that demanded the book be sealed. He probably believed that no one would ever escape from Hades to become the Redeemer and be found worthy to open the seals. God planned on sending out His church with the Gospel, but Satan probably demanded the right to stop the gospel using wars, famines, pestilences, and wild beasts. Jesus must open all the seals so that the trumpets can be sounded, to finally arrive at the 7th trumpet to get Satan dethroned.

Since all the seals are not opened yet, the book has not yet been opened. We would have no idea what was in the book, except John got to see it in his vision. The 70th-week will begin when Jesus opens the 7th seal. It will begin with the first trumpet judgment.

Remember, John's vision of the throne room in chapters 4 and 5 is the context of the first seal. Too many people wish to take the first seal out of this 32 AD context and place it somewhere in our future. They are 2000 years off in their theories. This is probably one of the most critical things to understand in Revelation: if people miss the context of the first seal, and imagine the first seal is the Antichrist coming in the future, then they will be in error on most of the rest of the book.

Some people are sure this first seal is to represent the Antichrist. This is impossible, and they are 2000 years off in their theory. They are thinking future while God was thinking past. They are pulling the first seal out of its early church context.

Consider the white horse of the first seal: John used the color white seventeen times in Revelation; every other time to represent righteousness. Would God choose the color white to represent evil one time out of seventeen—as if to represent the Antichrist? There is not a chance of this. Yet millions today imagine the rider on the white horse is the Antichrist. They have pulled the first seal out of its context and gone against John's common use of the color white.

Someone said for the first seal, "white represents deception"—the Antichrist imitating Christ. I think that is simply impossible. I will agree with this: if the Antichrist was to choose a color for himself, of course, he would choose white, but he did not get to choose his color in God's book. If we wish to see what color God chose for the Antichrist Beast, we look in chapter 17 and see that God chose fiery red. The point is, the Antichrist did not get to choose a color for himself—God chose his color as fiery red. For the first seal, God chose white to represent righteousness.

What then, did God consider as righteous on the earth around 32 AD? Only one thing: the church of Jesus Christ, having been washed in His blood. What did Isaiah write?

> 18. Come now, and let us reason together, saith the Lord: though your sins be as scarlet, they shall be as white as snow; though they be red like crimson, they shall be as wool. (King James Version, Isaiah 1)

The first seal is to represent the church, with the gospel of the Lord Jesus Christ, sent out to make disciples of all nations. The crown is to represent victory; complete and final victory. For example, this type of crown was awarded to a victor in the games. This does not fit the Antichrist. He will start victorious but will end in utter defeat. A victor's crown does not fit the Antichrist Beast. The bow in this rider's hand, that is a bow to shoot arrows, may represent the spiritual weapons of the church. The arrows would be the word of God.

There is no doubt that the church had to conquer: Satan was and still is the god of this world. He did not just step aside and allow the gospel to advance: the church had to overcome the principalities and powers over any new territory for the gospel to advance, but it was a spiritual battle.

Seal two, the red horse and rider; seal three, the black horse and rider; and seal four, the pale horse and rider; are to represent the devil and his attempts to stop the gospel; prevent it from advancing. However, God limited their theater of operation to only one-fourth of the earth. That one-fourth would certainly be centered on Jerusalem where the gospel began.

> 8. And I looked, and behold a pale horse: and his name that sat on him was Death, and Hell followed with him. And power was given unto them over the fourth part of the earth, to kill with sword, and with hunger, and with death, and with the beasts of the earth. (King James Version, Revelation 6)

Notice that these three riders ride together and that the white horse and rider are not with them. John wrote that power was given unto *"them."* John identifies them by the *sword*—the red horse and rider, *hunger*—the black horse and rider, and *death*—the pale horse and rider, with the white horse and rider left out of this group. He is righteous, the others are not. The white horse and rider rides alone, spreading the gospel, while these three ride together trying to stop the gospel. As we can see today, they failed. There are few places in the world where the gospel cannot be heard in some fashion.

There is one more problem with people imagining that the white horse and rider are to represent the Antichrist Beast of Revelation 13: if the first seal was the Antichrist, and the next three horsemen were his henchmen, then he would be limited to 1/4th the earth, which disagrees with other scriptures.

It is probable that these are not real horses with riders set out to accomplish these missions. It is much more likely they are symbolic in the vision to represent the mission of each.

The fifth seal is the first place we see any kind of waiting. It seems that Jesus broke or opened the first five seals as soon as He ascended, but stopped at the fifth seal, for at this seal there will be a long season of waiting. The church has waited, between the fifth and sixth seal, for almost 2000 years. John wrote that they must wait for the full number of martyrs to come in. There is a number, and God knows this number.

We could say it another way: God is waiting for the last martyr of the church age. The church age will end with the pre-tribulation rapture of the church, and the next moment after the rapture will be the start of the Day of the Lord and God's wrath.

The sixth seal begins the Day of the Lord or the Day of His wrath.

> 12. And I beheld when he had opened the sixth seal, and, lo, there was a great earthquake; and the sun became black as sackcloth of hair, and the moon became as blood;
>
> 17. For *the great day of his wrath is come*; and who shall be able to stand? (King James Version, Revelation 6)

The church—as seen in chapter 7 in the throne room of heaven, as the great crowd too large to number—is raptured before His wrath begins. The Day of his Wrath begins with a huge, worldwide earthquake. What causes this great earthquake? Notice this earthquake when God raised the elders when Jesus rose:

51. And, behold, the veil of the temple was rent in twain from the top to the bottom; and the earth did quake, and the rocks rent;

52. And the graves were opened; and many bodies of the saints which slept arose, (King James Version, Matthew 27)

When the graves were opened, there was a corresponding earthquake. I believe that when God brought together the particles of matter that once made up those saints' bodies, that resurrection event caused the great earthquake. It seems that these saints that rose when Jesus rose, were the elders of the Old Covenant. It is only a guess because God did not tell us. If it were the elders risen in Matthew 27, without a doubt, Adam was raised, as well as Abraham and Moses.

I think we can tell where in Revelation God will resurrect the Old Testament saints because that event will cause the world's worst earthquake. Jesus said He would raise them "on the last day," and the last day will be marked by the seventh vial: on the last 24 hour day of the 70th-week. At the seventh vial, we find the worst earthquake ever to hit the earth. It is so violent, the mountains shake down into the earth. Keep in mind, many of those resurrected then will be people from before the flood. The particles that once made up their bodies could be thousands of miles from their burial site. The flood would have changed almost everything. God will bring together those particles and once again it will be "their" body, but they will be bodies that will never die. Some experts believe the world population before the flood could have been in the billions of people. This resurrection is going to cause a huge earthquake.

Finally, in chapter 8 of Revelation, Jesus will open the

seventh and final seal, which will officially begin the 70th-week of Daniel. There will be 30 minutes of silence in heaven. Now, at last, the book that John saw in the Father's right hand will be opened and the events inside begin to take place.

CHAPTER 4

John's use of Parentheses

The Greeks certainly used parentheses, but the Greek language had no marks for parenthesis so John did not use any; we have to discover them by studying. Perhaps the easiest one to spot is the first five verses of chapter 12, which is talking about the birth of Christ and how Satan the dragon tried to kill Him as a child. If someone had written that in English today it would have been written as a parenthesis with the proper punctuation.

In John's narrative, the timing of chapter 12 is a moment after the abomination event Jesus talked about, marked by the seventh trumpet, that will stop the daily sacrifices and divide the week into two halves of 1260 days each. John never gives us the exact number of days for the first half of the week, but mentions the 1260 days twice for the second half. The fleeing of those in Judea (Revelation 12:6) will take place a moment after the abomination. Therefore chapter 12 is a midpoint chapter. However, the first five verses are about the birth of Christ and how the Dragon tried to kill Him as a child. John covered Jesus' entire life in one verse. John wrote these five verses as a parenthesis, having nothing to do with his narrative at the midpoint of the week.

For chronology we would read it like this, with verses 12:1–5 bracketed with parenthesis and indented:

> 11:19 And the temple of God was opened in heaven, and there was seen in his temple the ark of his testament: and there were lightnings, and voices, and thunderings, and an earthquake, and great hail.
>
> > (12:1 And there appeared a great wonder in heaven; a woman clothed with the sun, and the moon under her feet, and upon her head a crown of twelve stars:
> >
> > 2. And she being with child cried, travailing in birth, and pained to be delivered.
> >
> > 3. And there appeared another wonder in heaven; and behold a great red dragon, having seven heads and ten horns, and seven crowns upon his heads.
> >
> > 4. And his tail drew the third part of the stars of heaven, and did cast them to the earth: and the dragon stood before the woman which was ready to be delivered, for to devour her child as soon as it was born.
> >
> > 5. And she brought forth a man child, who was to rule all nations with a rod of iron: and her child was caught up unto God, and to his throne.)

6. And the woman fled into the wilderness, where she hath a place prepared of God, that they should feed her there a thousand two hundred and threescore days. (King James Version, Revelation 11 & 12)

John's chronology then goes from chapter 11 to chapter 12, verse 6, leaving those five verses out.

The Chapter 11 Problem of Chronology

Up to chapter 11, Revelation seems to be written quite chronologically. But this chapter has caused people many problems. Verse 2 gives us a 42-month countdown to the end of the week. Therefore, verse 2 must be at or very near the midpoint of the week. Then verse 3 gives us a 1260 day countdown, supposedly from the midpoint to the end of the week. Verse 3 also must be near the midpoint of the week, since it is the very next verse from the 42 month. So far the 1260 days flows well as the second half of the week, just like the 42 months. But then, John takes the reader down the complete 1260-day path of the Two Witnesses to their death and then resurrection. This makes it seem that the 7th trumpet would sound at the end of the week. What complicates this further is the next 1260-day countdown in chapter 12 that must also start at the midpoint of the week. It too is for the last half of the week. Some solve this dilemma by rearranging the Two Witness' testimony to the first half of the week. Is this what John had in mind? Not at all!

Here is another parenthesis most readers miss, found in chapter 11, about the two witnesses. Revelation chapter 11, verses 1 and 2, speak of the holy city (Jerusalem) being trampled for 42 months.

> 1. And there was given me a reed like unto a rod: and the angel stood, saying, Rise, and measure the temple of God, and the altar, and them that worship therein.

> 2. But the court which is without the temple leave out, and measure it not; for it is given unto the Gentiles: and the holy city shall they tread under foot *forty and two months*. (King James Version, Revelation 11)

I believe this shows us the man of sin's arrival in Jerusalem with his Gentile armies, just days before he will enter the temple and declare that he is God. He must of course be in Jerusalem if he is to enter the temple in Jerusalem. How did I come to this belief? I got this belief by revelation knowledge through meditating on these scriptures. I cannot prove this is the man of sin arriving in Jerusalem, but then, no one can prove it is not.

John tells us that Gentiles will trample the city for 42 months. I believe when the man of sin arrives in Jerusalem, he will arrive with his Gentile army, and they will trample the city. The next verse speaks of the arrival of the two witnesses, and how they will testify for 1260 days.

> 3. And I will give power unto my two witnesses, and they shall prophesy a thousand two hundred and threescore days, clothed in sackcloth. (King James Version, Revelation 11)

I believe the two witnesses show up then because the man of sin has just arrived in Jerusalem. John wrote the following verses, 11:4–14, as a parenthesis with no bearing on John's chronology, taking the readers down the last half of the week with the Two Witnesses. Most people miss this parenthesis and their chronology is then in error. They are forced to move the two witnesses' 1260 days to the first half of the week.

Backing up to verse 2 again, we read that Gentiles will trample the city for 42 months. This 42-month countdown will begin in verse 2, which is close to the midpoint, and will end just before the seventh vial that ends the week. The armies will move from Jerusalem to the valley for the coming battle.

Next, John tells us that the two witnesses will testify for 1260 days, starting at the same time as the trampling, just before the midpoint. Their count is in days, so it will be correct to the day. Their testimony will end just 3½ days before the end of the week when they will be killed.

I believe the text tells us that they will arrive in Jerusalem 3½ days before the abomination that divides the week and begin their testimony. God will "mark" the abomination with the sounding of the seventh trumpet. They will testify for 1260 days, which will take them to just 3½ days before the seventh vial that ends the week. Then they will lay dead for 3½ days, and finally be resurrected at the seventh vial. I believe that is when God will resurrect all the Old Testament saints. (Most people believe the two witnesses will be Old Testament saints.)

I believe they arrive right then, at the timing of verse 3, right after the start of the 42-month countdown, just 3½ days before the midpoint. They show up then because the man of sin just showed up. Since John does not tell us, perhaps there is some little time after the man of sin arrives until the two witnesses show up. However, since God will know the moment he arrives in Jerusalem, I believe the two witnesses will arrive at that same time or a moment later.

For John's chronology, the man of sin will arrive in Jerusalem perhaps a few days before the abomination event. I believe the abomination event Jesus talked about will be when the man of sin enters the temple and declares he is God. Of course, standing in the holiest place in the Jewish temple, his meaning will be clear: he is the God of the Jews. Jesus said: "When ye, therefore, shall see the abomination of desolation, spoken of by Daniel the prophet, stand in the holy place." Many translations say "standing." Notice that verse 11:3 is written just before the seventh trumpet that will mark the exact midpoint of the week.

If anyone other than the High Priest should enter the holiest place in the temple, it would pollute the temple and before the daily sacrifices continue, someone would have to cleanse the temple. This is what Daniel 9:27 tells us: the week will be divided by an event that will stop the daily sacrifices.

I believe that the two witnesses will arrive just moments after the man of sin arrives in Jerusalem. They will testify for 3½ days and then the man of sin will enter the temple and declare to the world that he is God, committing the abomination Jesus talked about. He will then be revealed as the Beast of Revelation or the Antichrist. The seventh trumpet will sound to mark that time in heaven. Then a second or two later, those living in Judea that see this abomination will begin to flee (12:6). The two witnesses will then testify almost to the end of the week.

If people do not recognize 11:4–13 as a parenthesis, and not a part of John's chronology, they will think the two witnesses must testify in the first half of the week. They are forced into concluding that the preceding verse, the start of the 42-month countdown, is for the last half of the week, but the next verse is for the first half of the week. That would be very clumsy writing. It is not the Author's intent at all. Only 3½ days of their testimony will be in the first half of the week. The Holy Spirit, the Author, intends that their testimony is in the second half of the 70th-week, parallel to the 42 months of trampling and the Beast's 42 of authority. Therefore verses 11:4-13 were written as a parenthesis. John takes us down a *side journey* with these Two Witnesses only, from the midpoint to the end of the week. Then in verse 15 John comes right back to the midpoint to sound the 7th trumpet. Some people solve this dilemma by believing that John begins a parenthesis with chapter 10, to include chapter 11 up to verse 13 or 14. That theory takes the 42 months of trampling and the 1260 days of witnessing out of John's chronology, so it cannot be the Author's intent.

Therefore, for chronology, the man of sin will enter Jerusalem with his Gentile armies, and the 42-month countdown for the trampling of Jerusalem will begin. Next, the two witnesses will arrive and begin their 1260 days of testimony. Then the man of sin will enter the temple and declare that he is God—which will be the abomination Jesus spoke of. Next, those in Judea will begin to flee the moment they see the man of sin declaring he is God.

For chronology we would read it as if the indented text were a parenthesis and the true chronology would be the standard text.

> 1. And there was given me a reed like unto a rod: and the angel stood, saying, Rise, and measure the temple of God, and the altar, and them that worship therein.

> 2. But the court which is without the temple leave out, and measure it not; for it is given unto

the Gentiles: and the holy city shall they tread under foot forty and two months.

3. And I will give power unto my two witnesses, and they shall prophesy a thousand two hundred and threescore days, clothed in sackcloth.

(4. These are the two olive trees, and the two candlesticks standing before the God of the earth.

5. And if any man will hurt them, fire proceedeth out of their mouth, and devoureth their enemies: and if any man will hurt them, he must in this manner be killed.

…

12. And they heard a great voice from heaven saying unto them, Come up hither. And they ascended up to heaven in a cloud; and their enemies beheld them.

13. And the same hour was there a great earthquake, and the tenth part of the city fell, and in the earthquake were slain of men seven thousand: and the remnant were affrighted, and gave glory to the God of heaven.)

14. The second woe is past; and, behold, the third woe cometh quickly.

15. And the seventh angel sounded; and there were great voices in heaven, saying, The kingdoms of this world are become the kingdoms of our Lord, and of his Christ, and he shall reign forever and ever. (King James Version, Revelation 11)

In chapter 12, we see that immediately after the seventh trumpet, those living in Judea begin fleeing, and at the same time, war breaks out in heaven. I suspect that the seventh trumpet will be Michael's signal to take Satan down, as well as mark the time of the abomination. At the seventh trumpet, the kingdoms of the world are given to Jesus Christ, the rightful owner. Satan's position as God of this world will have ended. This is why war breaks out in heaven at this time. The 6000-year lease Satan usurped from Adam will end, and suddenly Satan will have no more legal hold on earth. When two or more things happen at the same time, the writer can only write them one after another, but they may be happening simultaneously. I believe that the war in heaven will begin at the same time as those in Judea begin to flee.

After the war in heaven, God shows John in the vision what the dragon will do: immediately go after those who have fled from Judea. It will be Jews, for the most part, that live in Judea, so it will be Jews that flee. In failing to capture them, the Dragon will then turn and go after the "remnant" of the woman's seed. What could this mean? Jesus said, "salvation is of the Jews." Indeed it is, but because the Jews rejected Jesus as their Messiah, God turned to the Gentiles. The gentile church then could be seen as the "seed" of the woman, who is Israel. Why "remnant?" Because the pre-tribulation rapture will remove the "main load" previous to chapter 12. John is still writing of events just after the midpoint.

In chapter 13, John saw "the Beast" rise up from the waters. Remember, he will be "revealed" as the beast when he enters the temple and declares he is God. However, John could not write of several simultaneous events at the same time. He had to write them one after another. I believe the Beast rising in chapter 13 will come soon after he reveals himself as the Beast, by declaring he is God. In other words, there may be very little time from the 7th trumpet to the Beast rising.

John wrote,

> 5. And there was given unto him a mouth speaking great things and blasphemies, and power was given unto him to continue forty and two months. (King James Version, Revelation 13)

I believe John has another parenthesis in chapter 13, starting in verse 6 or 7 that takes us on another "side journey" down the last half of the week with the Beast and False Prophet, showing us what they will do during the last part of the week— exactly as he did with the two witnesses. This parenthesis will go to the end of the chapter.

John has shown us five events that begin at or near the midpoint and go to the end of the week. Make no mistake: all five are events for the last half of the week. In three of these events, he just gives us the verse to start the countdown, but in two of them, he takes the reader down the path of the last half of the week with a parenthesis.

There is another parenthesis in chapter 20.

> 4. And I saw thrones, and they sat upon them, and judgment was given unto them: and I saw

the souls of them that were beheaded for the witness of Jesus, and for the word of God, and which had not worshipped the beast, neither his image, neither had received his mark upon their foreheads or in their hands; and they lived and reigned with Christ a thousand years.

5. (But the rest of the dead lived not again until the thousand years were finished.) This is the first resurrection. (King James Version, Revelation 20)

When we consider the five mentions of the 3½ years, written in chapters 11 through 13, two written in days, two written in months and one written in "times," most readers would not consider the next verse for each mention would be after the 3½ years had finished. Most understand that the countdown to the end would begin at that verse where it is first mentioned, but not end in the same verse. For example, consider the 42 months of trampling the city as shown in 11:1–2. Most readers would not think that 11:3 would then be 42 months later. When people read of the 1260 days of fleeing given in 12:6, they don't believe that 12:7 is 1260 days later.

Most readers understand these countdowns as *starting* in the verse of mention and then counting down to the end of the week. Why then would readers consider the 1260 days of witnessing would be different? It is only because John took the readers down the last half of the week with the Two Witnesses as a side journey. These verses were certainly written as a parenthesis.

John uses Greek Aorist verbs all through His book, with an exception being here with the two witnesses. These Greek Aorist verbs are unusual because in some forms they show no tense at all: there is simply no timing information given in these undefined verbs. One Greek dictionary has "not inflected to show tense." The Aorist indicative mood shows us events started and finished in the past. (I am not a Greek scholar, but this is what I read.) Some of these verbs cannot be translated accurately into English, because all English verbs show tense.

An example would be at the sixth seal where John wrote "the great day of his wrath is come." Written in English it would seem to say "right now, at this time." However, in Greek, it indicates a past action.

In Revelation, we often have to decide timing by the verse of the first mention. The 6th seal is John's first mention of the Day of His wrath, so I believe that is where God's wrath will begin.

One place where John used future tense Greek verbs is when he described the two witnesses: in verse 11:3, "will give" and "shall prophesy" are future tense verbs. I think John used future tense here so people would know their testimony is in the future from this verse, not before. In other words, these future tense verbs make it impossible that their testimony, written near the midpoint, is for the first half of the week. They will testify from this point onward to the end of the week.

The first mention of the Two Witnesses is in 11:3. It would seem that verse shows us the moment that they suddenly appear. In John's narrative, that is just before the midpoint of the week. The way John wrote it, the reader should know that they suddenly appeared, right then in John's narrative, just after the 42 month countdown started. It would be totally out of character for John to mention them here near the midpoint when they showed up and began witnessing 1260 days before. All through Revelation John shows us timing by the first mention of something. Every mention of the 3½ year period of time is given in midpoint chapters: 11 through 13. Just that should tell every reader that each countdown would begin at or near the midpoint of the week. Yet, some people imagine that if the time is given in days, it is for the first half of the week, and if given in months, it is for the second half of the week. The truth is, every mention of a 3½ year countdown is for the last half of the week.

CHAPTER 5

Six Different Parallel Paths

In chapters 11 through 13, John begins five different countdowns to the end:

42 months of trampling:	Revelation 11:1–2,
1260 days of testifying:	Revelation 11:3,
1260 days of fleeing:	Revelation 12:6,
3½ years given as "time:"	Revelation 12:14,
42 months of authority:	Revelation 13:5.

These countdowns all begin close to the midpoint and will continue counting down to the end of the week. Remember the words Jesus spoke to me:

"Every time I mentioned an event that would begin at the midpoint and go to the end of the week, I always included the 3½ years. When you find the mentions of the 3½ years, you will be very close to the exact midpoint."

Because of Jesus' words, we know that every mention of the 3½ years represents an event starting at the midpoint and going to the end, whether given in days, months, or years. Without any doubt the 1260 days of testifying for the Two Witnesses fit into this category.

For two of these countdowns, John took us on a side journey down the rest of the week using a parenthesis. The first of these two is found in Chapter 11: the 1260 days of testifying; and the second is in chapter 13: the 42 months of authority. For the other three countdowns, John just gave us the proper time to start the countdown.

The first countdown is the 42 months that Gentiles will trample the city:

> 2. But the court which is without the temple leave out, and measure it not; for it is given unto the Gentiles: and the holy city shall they tread under foot forty and two months. (King James Version, Revelation 11)

The second countdown is the 1260 days of witnessing: My guess is, these two countdowns will begin at the same time or close:

> 3. And I will give power unto my two witnesses, and they shall prophesy a thousand two hundred and threescore days, clothed in sackcloth. (King James Version, Revelation 11)

The third countdown will start after the midpoint:

> 6. And the woman fled into the wilderness, where she hath a place prepared of God, that they should feed her there a thousand two hundred and threescore days. (King James Version, Revelation 12)

The fourth countdown will probably begin at the same time or shortly after the fleeing in verse 6:

> 14. And to the woman were given two wings of a great eagle, that she might fly into the wilderness, into her place, where she is nourished for a time, and times, and half a time, from the face of the serpent. (King James Version, Revelation 12)

The fifth and final countdown will be the last countdown to begin:

> 5. And there was given unto him a mouth speaking great things and blasphemies; and power was given unto him to continue forty and two months. (King James Version, Revelation 13)

Therefore, all five of these countdowns will be taking place, or counting down, *concurrently*—after their staggered beginning. In other words, while the Antichrist Beast is exercising his 42 months of authority, the "woman" will be supernaturally protected and fed, those in Judea who fled will continue fleeing, the two witnesses will continue witnessing, and the city will continue to be trampled— all taking place at the same time.

During chapters 14 and 15, all these countdowns are counting down towards the end simultaneously, and all but one will end in chapter 16. The ending of these five different countdowns is not written by John except for the 42 months of the authority of the Beast. John shows us that Jesus will capture the Beast and False when He returns, as shown in Revelation 19. We can guess the other four countdowns will end at or near the seventh trumpet that ends the week.

The point is, when five events are all happening at the same time, John cannot write of all events at the same time. He wrote them down in the order in which the different countdowns will begin. John couldn't write in perfect chronological order when events are simultaneous. To add more information to two of these countdowns, John used parentheses.

However, all this being said: in general, any event written in a given chapter will certainly take place after events of an earlier chapter and before the events of a later chapter. Any theory that must rearrange John's God-given order will be found as incorrect. For example, consider the seventh trumpet found in chapter 11. It will most certainly take place after the events of chapters 6, 7. 8, and 9. No angel will sound a trumpet until Jesus has opened all seven seals. The trumpets are written inside the book, and the book cannot be opened until Jesus has opened all seven seals.

We find Jesus coming in glory and power in Revelation 19. Yet, some people imagine He comes at the seventh trumpet. There is no coming at the seventh trumpet. The courtroom in heaven will transfer the kingdoms of the world to Jesus at the seventh trumpet, but Jesus does not return to earth and take physical possession then. We find His coming in Revelation 19.

Other people imagine a coming at the sixth seal. They are almost right. Some imagine this because they imagine the sixth seal will take place at the same moment as the seventh vial that ends the week. Jesus does not come at the seventh vial either. Others think the people *see* the face of God—so imagine He must have come. The truth of scripture is that He will come just before the 6th seal for the rapture of the church, which will then trigger the Day of His wrath (the day of the Lord) which begins at the 6th seal. Will the people see His face? It is doubtful because He will be hidden in a cloud. They will have seen all the signs for the Day of the Lord, so they know it has come. They could well imagine His face in wrath.

Many others imagine He will come at the seventh vial that ends the week. Yet, we find events written in chapters 17 through 19 that must take place before He returns to earth. These events will certainly take place at or after the seventh vial, but before Jesus returns in chapter 19. For example, Jesus does not return to earth until after the marriage and supper that will take place in heaven.

Another example: in chapter 19 we see that all the participants of the marriage and marriage supper are already in heaven. Yet, many people believe in a post-trib' rapture of the church. They don't realize there would be no way for them to get to heaven for the marriage. For some then, they rearrange and rewrite the scriptures in their minds, to fit their theory: those that believe in a post-trib' rapture must place the marriage and supper after His coming in power, and place it on earth—rearranging the written word of God. John places the marriage and supper in heaven before Christ returns to earth.

A case in point: when John wrote "Blessed are they which are called unto the marriage supper of the Lamb," we all know that a marriage supper comes after a marriage ceremony. If it is time for the marriage supper, that tells us the marriage is over. It is far better to form doctrine from the word of God as written, not rewrite scripture to fit a doctrine.

John shows us both the marriage and the marriage supper will take place in heaven, and then after these are finished, Jesus will descend with the armies of heaven. Remember the scripture in Daniel 12, after the saint in linen told Daniel that "to the end of these wonders" will be time, times and half of time, (3½ years)? The angel then gives Daniel another number: 1290 days: an event coming 30 days after the end of the week.

Jesus may return then. We cannot be dogmatic because neither Daniel or John tells us. We are told that no man knows the day nor the hour.

What then is the sixth parallel path? We have already discussed the five parallel paths that are countdowns to the end. John, however, had to write of those five in the order given him in the vision. The sixth path is John's narrative as he takes us from the midpoint to the end of the week.

Keep in mind, although there are five countdowns to the end, all counting down simultaneously, John mentions the beginning of each one and the countdown is then running in the background as John takes us through the last half of the week, to the seventh vial that ends the week.

It may at first appear that the Beast kills the two witnesses before the 7th trumpet that marks the midpoint, but when we discover John's parenthesis in Revelation 11, even their 1260 days goes almost to the end of the week.

CHAPTER 6

Observations, Warnings, and Prophecy

Chapter 14 is perhaps more difficult than other chapters when considering chronology. John begins by showing us the 144,000 that were sealed in chapter 7, but this time, John saw them in heaven. Did they get raptured? John does not tell us. If they did, when did they get raptured? Again, we don't know because John did not tell us. What is John's timing in chapter 14?

I believe John is just after the midpoint, but how long after we cannot tell. There are still things John must cover before the days of great tribulation get started. For timing then, I put chapter 14 "just after" the midpoint.

Next, John saw three angels with three different messages to give to all people in their native language, so all will understand. The first angel's message is simple: "fear God and worship Him." God called this message "the everlasting gospel." Notice that the gospel here in Revelation does not speak of Christ's death, burial, and resurrection, as Paul's gospel does—perhaps because the church age is over. This is the gospel for this time: only fear God and worship Him. Notice that Jesus as the Son is not even mentioned.

The next angel's message is that "Babylon is fallen, is

fallen." Why two "fallen's?" John does not tell us. It is given as a prophecy—foretelling coming events—because Babylon still exists at this time, at the midpoint of the week, and will continue to exist until the end of the week. I can only guess that one "fallen" is for the physical city of Jerusalem being taken. The other fallen may be "mystery" Babylon destroyed, the "mystery" city (Jerusalem) that will deceive the entire world while the Beast and False Prophet are living there.

Then a third angel has another sobering message: to worship the Beast or His image or to receive the mark of the Beast will doom someone to fire and brimstone forever and ever, in the presence of the Lamb and of the angels.

This last message is sobering, but we can assume, just as the first message, that it will be given to all people in their language so all will be without excuse. John wrote, "to every nation, and kindred, and tongue, and people." All through church history some people have tried to sit on the fence between going all out for God, or just trying to avoid the lake of fire; in other words, trying to avoid any decision. During the days of great tribulation, God will not allow any fence-sitters. The circumstances will force all people to choose a side: either God's side or the devil's side. No one will be in doubt about which side they are choosing.

Next, John wrote:

> 12. Here is the patience of the saints: here are they that keep the commandments of God, and the faith of Jesus.

> 13. And I heard a voice from heaven saying unto me, Write, Blessed are the dead which die in the Lord from henceforth: Yea, saith the Spirit, that they may rest from their labours; and their

works do follow them. (King James Version, Revelation 14)

These verses hint at the timing of the start of "the days" of "great tribulation." (Quotes from Matthew 24) I believe John is telling us, the image is now created, and people will now be forced to worship this image or be put to death. The mark is now ready to be enforced, and if people refuse the mark, they will be put to death. It seems the best thing to do for believers at this time is just to turn themselves in, lose their head, and become a martyr. The longer one tries to hide, and the longer one goes without water, the more pressure they will have, to take the mark.

The next verses John wrote are some of the most difficult for me to understand.

> 14. And I looked, and behold a white cloud, and upon the cloud one sat like unto the Son of man, having on his head a golden crown, and in his hand a sharp sickle.

> 15. And another angel came out of the temple, crying with a loud voice to him that sat on the cloud, Thrust in thy sickle, and reap: for the time is come for thee to reap; for the harvest of the earth is ripe.

> 16. And he that sat on the cloud thrust in his sickle on the earth; and the earth was reaped. (King James Version, Revelation 14)

Notice that this seems to be a harvest of the righteous.

Compare this with the next verses, which seem to be the harvest of the sinner.

> 17. And another angel came out of the temple which is in heaven, he also having a sharp sickle.

> 18. And another angel came out from the altar, which had power over fire; and cried with a loud cry to him that had the sharp sickle, saying, Thrust in thy sharp sickle, and gather the clusters of the vine of the earth; for her grapes are fully ripe.

> 19. And the angel thrust in his sickle into the earth, and gathered the vine of the earth, and cast it into the great winepress of the wrath of God.

> 20. And the winepress was trodden without the city, and blood came out of the winepress, even unto the horse bridles, by the space of a thousand and six hundred furlongs. (King James Version, Revelation 14)

This second harvest comes with wrath, while the previous one does not. John gives us a hint with the previous "Babylon is fallen, is fallen" that these verses should be taken as prophecy, not a statement of events taking place right at this place in John's narrative. Babylon gets destroyed in chapters 17 and 18, not in chapter 14. The Beast and False Prophet are taken in chapter 19, not in chapter 14.

Jesus describes a harvest In Mark.

26. And he said, So is the kingdom of God, as if a man should cast seed into the ground;

27. And should sleep, and rise night and day, and the seed should spring and grow up, he knoweth not how.

28. For the earth bringeth forth fruit of herself; first the blade, then the ear, after that the full corn in the ear.

29. But when the fruit is brought forth, immediately he putteth in the sickle, because the harvest is come. (King James Version, Mark 4)

Notice that in verse 29, a sickle is mentioned because it is harvest time. By this time in John's narrative, God is declaring that it is harvest time. The days of great tribulation have begun, and then, some unknown time after, the vials of God's wrath will be poured out. The week will end at the seventh vial where the worst earthquake this world has ever seen will hit: destroying every city in the world. After that, the battle of Armageddon, where millions will be harvested. God is using John to remind us that shortly after the midpoint of the week, the great harvest will begin.

These verses are symbolic and are prophetic at the same time: showing us that as people refuse the mark—lose their head—and show up in heaven— it is a harvest of the righteous. It will begin here but continue until the vials of God's wrath *shorten* those days of great tribulation and render the armies of the Beast incapable of doing anything.

Then the harvest of the sinners with wrath is a prophetic view of the judgment of the sinners. It will include the coming battle of Armageddon where millions of soldiers will be killed. It could also include the parable of the tares, where the wicked are taken. The "winepress" is symbolic. The blood to the horse's bridle may be real. We know God is not going to harvest humans with sickles. It is symbolic. At the time John wrote, sickles were used for harvest.

Many people imagine these events—the two harvests—happen in the time frame of chapter 14. I disagree because I find them happening later on in the book. Therefore I believe these events are written here as prophecy, looking forward in time to future events.

It would be silly to imagine God would warn people not to take the mark long after the mark was being enforced. Therefore, we can be assured that at the time in John's narrative that God gives the warning, the beast is not yet putting people to death for refusing the mark. We don't see the beheaded show up in heaven until chapter 15. Therefore, the days of great tribulation that Jesus spoke of will not begin until after the warning God gives here in chapter 14.

CHAPTER 7

Numbered Events of Revelation

There are several series of numbered events in Revelation, numbered by John for the proper sequencing. These numbered events make a timeline in the book of Revelation. It is ludicrous to think one could or should rearrange any of John's numbered events to fit a theory, yet people do.

The Seven Seals

The seals are sealing a book, preventing the book from being opened until all seven of the seals are opened first. Many readers concentrate on the seals and forget the book. John does not give us any history of this book except what we read, but I guess that Satan, as the prince and spiritual leader of this world, demanded the book be sealed and these seals must be opened before God could begin the 70th-week. He probably demanded that these seals could only be opened by a man who could escape death and escape from Hades. My guess is, he figured that no man would ever escape out of Hades, so he would remain as God of this world forever. It is only a guess, for John does not tell us. What we can surmise is, this book is a legal document created in heaven. Unless a man could be found worthy to take the book and open the first seal, God could not legally send out the church with the gospel to the nations, much less take the kingdoms of the world from Satan and give them to Jesus Christ.

The book itself seems to contain the 70th-week of Daniel: chapters 8 through 16 in Revelation. Once the seventh seal is opened, the book is opened and the next events in Revelation are the trumpet judgments. These trumpet judgments seem to be the first events written inside the book once it is opened. John did not tell us this in so many words, but there is a strong hint that this is true and this author is convinced of it. Many readers forget the book once the seals are opened, thinking the seals are all there is to the book, but this is a big mistake. It is this book that gets Satan removed as the God of this world.

The timing of the first seals is made clear from the context of chapters 4 and 5, but people continue to pull the first seal out of its early church context. They either don't understand the Author's intent or ignore chapters 4 and 5 completely. God put those chapters in so we would know about "the book;" how it was first seen in the hand of the Father, waiting for Jesus to ascend, get the book, and begin opening the seals. Without any doubt, the first seals were opened as soon as Jesus got the book into His hands.

The first five seals are the church age, up to the end of this age. It will end with the pre-tribulation rapture of the church, followed instantly by the sixth seal. The age of grace will end, and the Day of the Lord will begin. Grace ends; wrath begins.

The fifth seal gives us a hint as to where the rapture would be in Revelation, had John written of it. He did not see the rapture so he did not write of it. This seal is for the martyrs of the church age. They are told they must wait for judgment until the final number of martyrs has come in.

What would cause a martyr of the church age to be the last martyr? Of course, if the church age ends, there could be no more martyrs in the church age. The next martyr would be a Day of the Lord martyr or a 70th-week martyr. The moment of the rapture of the church, the last church age martyr will have come in, the Day of His wrath will begin, and the judgment that the martyrs were asking about, will begin.

Someone might wonder, "how do we know the fifth seal is for the church age and not the 70th-week?" Many people imagine, in error, that the first seal is the antichrist and these are martyrs from the days of great tribulation Jesus spoke of. The truth is, John has not yet even started the 70th-week, much less arrived in the second half of the week where the days of great tribulation will take place. We cannot take the first seal out of its first-century context. Most readers just ignore or miss the message of chapters 4 and 5: the vision of the throne room— and the search for one worthy to open the seals—forget that nearly 2000 years have passed, and want to make the first seals into future events, future to us even today. It is easy to see in the book of Revelation where the days of great tribulation begin: in chapter 15 John tells us the beheaded are beginning to show up in heaven. Most people want to rush things in Revelation. Some even suggest the days of great tribulation that Jesus spoke of are in the first seals, while John places them after chapter 14.

After the fifth seal, the next event John writes of is the sixth seal which begins God's judgment and wrath. This shows us clearly that the rapture must come after the fifth seal and before the sixth seal. The church has been waiting between these two seals every since the beginning of the church age. This is in perfect agreement with Paul in 1 Thessalonians chapter 5 where he gives us the timing of the rapture as just before the Day of the Lord and God's wrath.

The Seven Trumpet Judgments

The trumpet judgments come with God's wrath. They are the opening salvos of the Day of the Lord and the 70th-week of Daniel. Some people think God's wrath begins here with the first trumpet judgment. I think his wrath starts with the sixth seal. I would not argue either way. From the sixth seal to the seventh seal where the trumpets begin is probably only a few days. If the rapture comes on the "last trump" of the Feast of Trumpets, as many think, then it would be the "ten days of awe" to the seventh seal and start of the 70th-week.

Only one of the trumpet judgments gives the duration: five long months. It is the duration of the judgment of the stinging locusts. It is also the first woe. Since the seventh trumpet marks the midpoint, then the first six trumpet judgments will take the entire 42 months of the first half of the week. If each trumpet judgment lasted five months, that would be only 30 months (five months times six trumpets equals thirty), not 42 months that will make up a half week. Therefore some judgments must last longer than five months. We don't know the duration of the other trumpet judgments, because John did not tell us.

> 6. Howl ye; for the day of the Lord is at hand; it shall come as a destruction from the Almighty

> 9. Behold, the day of the Lord cometh, cruel both with wrath and fierce anger, to lay the land desolate: and he shall destroy the sinners thereof out of it. (King James Version, Isaiah 13)

Notice what God plans to accomplish during the Day of the Lord: to destroy the land, and to destroy the sinners living there. Now think about the first trumpet judgments:

7. The first angel sounded, and there followed hail and fire mingled with blood, and they were cast upon the earth: and the third part of trees was burnt up, and all green grass was burnt up. (King James Version, Revelation 8)

Is that "laying the land desolate?" Destroying a third of the trees and all the grass is certainly a beginning to laying the land desolate.

8. And the second angel sounded, and as it were a great mountain burning with fire was cast into the sea: and the third part of the sea became blood;

9. And the third part of the creatures which were in the sea, and had life, died; and the third part of the ships were destroyed.

10. And the third angel sounded, and there fell a great star from heaven, burning as it were a lamp, and it fell upon the third part of the rivers, and upon the fountains of waters; (King James Version, Revelation 8)

We see the destruction of the earth continuing with one-third of all water being turned to blood. People often wonder, is this worldwide, localized to the Middle East, or perhaps only to Israel? John does not tell us. Since sinners are found worldwide, it would seem these judgments will be worldwide. It is only a guess. Please take note, that many of the verses about the Day of the Lord speak of God's wrath. We can see that the trumpet judgments are fulfilling what God said He would do during the

Day of the Lord: destroy the earth. It is plain then that these judgments are indeed a part of the Day of the Lord, fulfilling those scriptures, so come with God's wrath.

Why is this important? Many people imagine the Day of the Lord does not begin until Jesus comes to the battle of Armageddon. It is only imagination. John shows us clearly that the Day of the Lord, or the Day of His wrath, begins at the sixth seal and continues through the book. This is no problem for some; they just move the 6th seal to the end of the week. Their theory will be wrong.

The sixth trumpet judgment is the 2nd woe. It is indeed a woe, for this one judgment will kill one-third of the earth's population. It is a severe judgment. I have wondered if this is the parable of the tares coming to pass. John does not tell us, but I cannot find any other judgment in Revelation that looks like the parable of the tares.

The seventh trumpet is the third and last woe. Not because events happen at that moment, but because it will be at the seventh trumpet that Satan is cast down.

> 12. Therefore rejoice, ye heavens, and ye that dwell in them. *Woe* to the inhabiters of the earth and of the sea. for the devil is come down unto you, having great wrath, because he knoweth that he hath but a short time. (King James Version, Revelation 12) (Emphasis added)

Notice that John says "woe" to those left alive on earth. This is the third woe that comes with the sounding of the seventh trumpet. This seventh trumpet will be Michael's cue to go to war with Satan and cast him down. He is cast down with great wrath.

Many people imagine that the seventh trumpet is Paul's

"last trump," pointing out that it is the last trumpet in the bible. Indeed, Paul's "last trump" is the last trumpet of a series, but it is certainly NOT this series listed in Revelation. First, Paul's trump is the trump of God, meaning that God will sound this trumpet. We can easily see that angels sound the trumpets in Revelation. Next, there is no gathering at the seventh trumpet. It is the event that marks the exact midpoint of the week. There is no "coming" here. There is a legal transaction that takes place in the courtroom of heaven: the kingdoms of the world are taken from Satan and given to Jesus Christ—the rightful owner.

It is extremely likely that Paul's "last trump" is the last trumpet in the series of trumpets at the Feast of Trumpets. That feast will be the next feast fulfilled by Jesus when He comes for His church. It will also be the last trumpet sound of the church age.

What does happen at the seventh trumpet? First, it is the "marker" (God's word, not mine) for the midpoint. The angel will sound the seventh trumpet the moment the man of sin enters the temple and declared he is the God of the Jews. However, the seventh trumpet will accomplish more than that. Michael, the Arc Angel has been waiting for that seventh trumpet for a long time. When he hears it, that will be his signal to go to war with Satan and the demons—to drive them out of the heavenly sphere and down to earth. Satan will be cast down. Why will this happen at the seventh trumpet? What is this great secret that will happen then?

> 6. And sware by him that liveth for ever and ever, who created heaven, and the things that therein are, and the earth, and the things that therein are, and the sea, and the things which are therein, that there should be time no longer:

> 7. But in the days of the voice of the seventh
> angel, when he shall begin to sound, *the mystery*
> *of God should be finished*, as he hath declared to
> his servants the prophets. (King James Version,
> Revelation 10) (Emphasis added)

"Time no longer" is better translated as no more delay in time. The mystery is about how God will end Satan's reign as god or prince of this planet. It seems God gave Adam a 6000-year lease on this planet. It seems God decreed that man would rule the earth for 6000 years, then God would rule the earth for the seventh thousand years. This is what ancient Hebrews believed.

The point is, when the seventh trumpet sounds, it will mark the end of the 6000 years of man's rule on earth. One millennium ends and another begins. God finally gets His planet back. Make no mistake though: Jesus will not immediately take possession: He has given the Beast 42 months to reign. This is not the start of the thousand-year reign of Christ. Satan is not yet bound. The thousand-year reign of Christ will start after Satan is bound, as shown in Revelation chapter 20.

The vials of God's wrath

The vials will be poured out at the peak of the Beast's murder regime. God must cut these days of great tribulation short, as He said. He will shorten the days of great tribulation by pouring out the vials. These will render the armies of the Beast incapable of doing much of anything.

It seems many have not understood: there will be 42 months of authority given to the beast: that is written in God's word and will never change. It is not the 42 months that change. The

70th-week will remain the same—2520 days in length. What people miss is, there will be "days" of great tribulation during the last half of the week. In other words, God did not put a title to the last half of the week as "the great tribulation." However, people have added that title. It is the number of days of great tribulation or great pressure that people will feel during the last half of the week that will be shortened. Days will continue up to the complete 42 months of the Beast's authority, but they will no longer be days of great tribulation. They will probably be dark days of fear, wondering what will come next.

The image will not be created until the False Prophet shows up.

> 11. And I beheld *another beast* coming up out of the earth; and he had two horns like a lamb, and he spake as a dragon.
>
> 12. And he exerciseth all the power of the first beast before him, and causeth the earth and them which dwell therein to worship the first beast, whose deadly wound was healed.
>
> 13. And he doeth great wonders, so that he maketh fire come down from heaven on the earth in the sight of men,
>
> 14. And deceiveth them that dwell on the earth by the means of those miracles which he had power to do in the sight of the beast; *saying to them that dwell on the earth, that they should make an image to the beast*, which had the wound by a sword, and did live. (King James Version, Revelation 13) (Emphasis added)

Notice that the image will not be created until the False Prophet enters the scene. However, John does not tell us how long after the Antichrist beast is revealed until this False Prophet shows up. One thing we can be sure of: God will warn the people about the mark *before* it will be enforced.

The seventh vial ends the 70th-week. Notice there is a huge earthquake—the worst ever to hit planet earth. It is so violent that the mountains shake down into the earth and are seen no more, and the islands disappear.

It is at the seventh vial that God will raise the Old Testament saints. It will be the raising of those before the flood that will cause this violent shaking. The particles that once made up those human bodies before the flood may well be scattered around the planet due to the flood. However in one instant of time, God will bring those particles together and form those bodies just as they were when they died. This will cause a tremendous earthquake. Jesus said several times that He would raise them (the Jews and Hebrews) on the "last day." The seventh vial will be poured out on the last 24 hour day of the 70th-week.

Notice in chapter 11, the story of the Two Witnesses: verses 11:4 through 11:13 are written as a parenthesis: the earthquake shown there, where the Witnesses are raised, is this same earthquake seen at the seventh vial. It will end the "70th-week" of Daniel.

This is NOT the day Jesus returns to earth. Daniel 12 mentions an event to happen on day 1290: 30 days after the 70th week comes to an end—so 30 days after day 1260 counting from the midpoint to the end. Could this be His return to Armageddon?

CHAPTER 8

God's Sequence of Events After the 70th Week

The 70th-week of Daniel—the close of the Jewish age—will end with the seventh vial. Many people imagine Jesus will return on that day. They are mistaken. If Jesus did return on the 1260th day from the abomination, then everyone could count down from the abomination and know the exact day He would come. The truth is, no one will know the day nor the hour, either for His coming *for* His church as written by Paul in 1 Thessalonians. 4 & 5, or His coming *with* His church as written in Revelation 19.

The first things we see after the seventh vial has ended the week, are the events of chapters 17 and 18: the destruction of the kingdom of the Beast and the "mystery Babylon" which is the "mystery" city of Jerusalem—a city from where the Beast and False Prophet deceive the entire world. The physical city will be destroyed but will be rebuilt; it will never, ever again be a city from where deception will come. It will never again be a mystery city, related to Sodom and Egypt.

Chapters 17 and 18 tell us about the destruction of "Mystery, Babylon The Great, The Mother Of Harlots And Abominations Of The Earth." Notice who John tells us she is: the Author's meaning of the great "Mystery, Babylon."

3. So he carried me away in the spirit into the wilderness: and I saw *a woman* sit upon a scarlet coloured beast, full of names of blasphemy, having seven heads and ten horns.

18. And the woman which thou sawest is *that great city*, which reigneth over the kings of the earth. (King James Version, Revelation 17) (Emphasis added)

8. And there followed another angel, saying, Babylon is fallen, is fallen, *that great city*, because she made all nations drink of the wine of the wrath of her fornication. (King James Version, Revelation 14) (Emphasis added)

As you see, John refers to "Babylon" as "that great city" in chapter 14. Notice that John tells us who this woman is to represent: "that great city." Yet, many still imagine John is talking about all false religions, or perhaps one well-known religion. John tells us plainly that "the woman" is "that great city." Does John tell us what "great city" he is talking about? Of course He does—in chapter 14.

8. And their dead bodies shall lie in the street of the great city, which spiritually is called Sodom and Egypt, where also our Lord was crucified. (James Version, Revelation 11)

I cannot see much difference in "that great city," and "the great city." I think John is talking about the same city. As you can see, in chapter 11 John identifies this "great city" as the city in which Jesus was crucified. In other words, He is talking about Jerusalem. Why then would God call the city of Jerusalem "Sodom and Egypt" and "Mystery" Babylon?

It has always been God's plan that the city of Jerusalem would point people *to* God. It was that way in the days of Solomon. But Jerusalem is where the Beast and False Prophet will reign over their kingdom. It will be from the city of Jerusalem that the Beast and False Prophet will deceive the entire world. No false religion in the past has even come close to deceiving the entire world. Not even all false religions together have come close to deceiving the entire world.

John begins chapter 19 in verse 2 by telling us that God has judged "Mystery Babylon." John gives us no indication of any time passing during chapters 17 and 18. Perhaps there is no time there; John is just showing us the destruction which will come at the seventh vial. We cannot be sure because John does not tell us.

Next, after much praise, John tells us that the time for the marriage has come. That is, right then, at the time of that verse: not later, not on earth, but in heaven at the time of this verse. John is just giving us the highlights.

After the marriage, John tells us the time for the marriage supper has come. Again, right then at the reading of the verse. We can be sure, if it is time for the supper, that the marriage ceremony has finished. A marriage supper comes after the marriage ceremony. This is another proof these events take place in heaven, just before Jesus descends to Armageddon.

How much time will have passed since the seventh vial that ended the week? We can only guess because John did not tell us. However, in Daniel 12 we learn that an event will take place 30 days after the week has ended on the 1260th day. In other words, the week will end on the 1260th day, but then 30 days later, on the 1290th day, an important event will occur. Perhaps it is His return to earth. This would leave 30 days for the marriage and supper. It is only a guess because "no one knows the day nor the hour" of His coming.

> 11. And from the time that the daily sacrifice shall be taken away, and the abomination that maketh desolate set up, there shall be a thousand two hundred and *ninety days*. (King James Version, Daniel 12)

Daniel had asked "O my Lord, what shall be the end of these *things*?" The man in linen answered as we see in verse 11. From the time the daily sacrifice is taken away, which is the same time the abomination is set up — from that time — it will be 1290 days to the "end of these things." In other words, the week will end, but other things take place up to this point in time, 30 days after the week will end. I believe that Jesus will return on that 1290th day. However, John does not tell us what event will happen then, only that "the end of these things" will arrive. "Things" is an added word, so Daniel was asking the same question as someone previously had asked, how long "to the end of these wonders."

Many people believe this verse 11 is a "from" - "to" statement: *from* the time "the daily sacrifice is taken away" *to* the time "the abomination is set up..." They are mistaken. It is not that kind of a sentence. In context, the "from" is in verse 12:1; from the time of great tribulation to the end would be time, times and half of time or 3 ½ years. But this is an imprecise starting time: In verse 11 God is giving Daniel a clear starting time. It is the very same starting time we see in the New Testament: at the 7th trumpet when the man of sin enters the temple and declares He is God. Without a doubt, He will place an image of some kind there at that same time, probably of himself. It will be at that time that the 1290 day countdown will begin.

Make no mistake: the marriage and supper will take place *in heaven* some unknown time after the seventh vial that ends the week. Some might wonder why this marriage and marriage supper did not take place right after the rapture. I can only guess, for John does not tell us; God has to wait for the resurrection of the Old Testament saints that will take place on the last 24 hour day of the 70th-week – at the 7th vial, at the time of the terrible earthquake.

Some may wonder where in Revelation the millennium we are now in changes to the next millennium. I believe that event is at the 7th trumpet when Adam's 6000-year lease ends. In other words, at the 7th trumpet one millennium ends and the next begins. The 1000 year reign of Christ will begin right at the 7th trumpet where it is written that "The kingdoms of this world are become the kingdoms of our Lord, and of his Christ; and he shall *reign* for ever and ever." (Revelation 11:15) It is only a guess, but I think John hints strongly of this. Why are the kingdoms taken from Satan and given to Jesus then and not any time sooner or later? There must be a legal reason it will occur at that time.

Christ's Return to earth

After the marriage and supper, Jesus will get on a white horse and descend to earth, with the armies of Heaven with Him—all on white horses.

> 14. And the armies which were in heaven followed him upon white horses, clothed in fine

linen, white and clean. (King James Version, Revelation 19)

I fully expect that the church will be included in one of the armies of heaven. He will descend to the Battle of Armageddon. His descent will come AFTER the marriage and supper in heaven.

Battle of Armageddon

12. And the sixth angel poured out his vial upon the great river Euphrates; and the water thereof was dried up, that the way of *the kings of the east* might be prepared.

13. And I saw three unclean spirits like frogs come out of the mouth of the dragon, and out of the mouth of the beast, and out of the mouth of the false prophet.

14. For they are the spirits of devils, working miracles, which *go forth unto the kings of the earth and of the whole world*, to gather them to the battle of that great day of God Almighty. (King James Version, Revelation 16) (Emphasis added)

Notice what John wrote: "the whole world." It would seem that the combined armies of every nation of the world that has a standing army, will assemble in Israel. There are around seventy nations in the world with at least a hundred thousand or greater number of troops: army and reserves plus paramilitary. At least these seventy nations may send troops to Israel.

It is almost certain that none of the troops will know that they are assembling to fight with the God of creation. They will be told a lie. Perhaps they will be told they are coming to wipe Israel off the map forever.

John does not give us much information about the actual battle—because there won't be much of a battle.

> 19. And I saw the beast, and the kings of the earth, and their armies, gathered together to make war against him that sat on the horse, and against his army.
>
> 20. And *the beast was taken, and with him the false prophet* that wrought miracles before him, with which he deceived them that had received the mark of the beast, and them that worshipped his image. These both were cast alive into a lake of fire burning with brimstone.
>
> 21. And *the remnant were slain with the sword of him that sat upon the horse,* which sword proceeded out of his mouth: and all the fowls were filled with their flesh. (King James Version, Revelation 19) (Emphasis added)

From Joel:

> 2. I will also gather all nations, and will bring them down into the valley of Jehoshaphat, and will plead with them there for my people and for my heritage Israel, whom they have scattered

among the nations, and parted my land. (King James Version, Joel 3)

From Zachariah:

2. For I will gather all nations against Jerusalem to battle; and the city shall be taken, and the houses rifled, and the women ravished; and half of the city shall go forth into captivity, and the residue of the people shall not be cut off from the city.

3. Then shall the Lord go forth, and fight against those nations, as when he fought in the day of battle. (King James Version, Zachariah 14)

From Zephaniah :

7. Hold thy peace at the presence of the Lord God: for the day of the Lord is at hand: for the Lord hath prepared a sacrifice, he hath bid his guests. (King James Version, Zephaniah 1)

From these verses, it would seem to be a short battle. They also show us that the Beast and False prophet will be there with the armies, but will be taken and thrown into the lake of fire.

Into the Millennial Reign of Christ

The next thing John shows us is Satan being bound for 1000 years. We don't see the official start of the millennial kingdom. John shows us a picture of the earthly reign of Christ after it has begun.

4. And I saw *thrones,* and *they sat upon them,* and judgment was given unto them: and I saw *the souls of them that were beheaded* for the witness of Jesus, and for the word of God, and which had not worshipped the beast, neither his image, neither had received his mark upon their foreheads, or in their hands; and they lived and reigned with Christ a thousand years.

5. (But the rest of the dead lived not again until the thousand years were finished.) This is the first resurrection. (King James Version, Revelation 20) (Parenthesis and emphasis added)

Who would be on those thrones, as judges? It would be the Old Testament and New Testament saints who at this time will have their resurrection bodies.

6. Blessed and holy is he that hath part in the first resurrection: on such the second death hath no power, but *they shall be priests of God and of Christ, and shall reign with him* a thousand years. (James Version, Revelation 20)(Emphasis added)

Take careful notice: all those who take part in the "first" or most honorable resurrection will reign with Christ. John has another parenthesis in verse 5. The "first resurrection" goes with "they lived and reigned with Christ..." John then jumps over the entire 1000 year reign of Christ in one verse:

> 7. And when the thousand years are expired, Satan shall be loosed out of his prison. (King James Version, Revelation 20)

After the 1000 year reign of Christ, God will allow Satan to be loosed for a time and he, Satan, will deceive millions again. There will probably be billions born during these thousand years, but none of them will have been tested. It seems many will fail this test and will side with Satan and be destroyed.

When the fire comes down from heaven and destroys them, Satan is then cast into the lake of fire. It is a one-way trip. It will be forever. Now, after the thousand years, it is time for the resurrection and judgment of the wicked:

> 5. But the rest of the dead lived not again *until the thousand years were finished*…(King James Version, Revelation 20)

God will resurrect all the wicked for the great, White Throne Judgment. It will be the final resurrection mentioned in the bible. There are only two resurrections mentioned: one will be for all the righteous, the second for all the unrighteous.

Even with these several mentions of the 1000 year reign of Christ on earth, many cannot believe it. I have read online, quotes from "ancient Jewish sages," perhaps from the time of Moses, that since God created for 6 days and rested on the 7th, then mankind would rule the world for 6000 years, and God would rule the world for the 7th thousand years. The book of Revelation confirms this is true. God will, indeed, rule the earth for a thousand years.

The end of our Heaven and Earth

> 11. And I saw a great white throne, and him
> that sat on it, from whose face *the earth and the*
> *heaven fled away; and there was found no place*
> *for them.* (King James Version, Revelation 20)
> (Emphasis added)

> At the time of the White Throne Judgment, the
> planet we live on will be gone forever. Read it
> carefully: "there was found no place for them."

Without any doubt, there will be righteous left on the earth, as well as the unrighteous. Will they take part in this resurrection? John wrote, "I saw the dead, small and great, stand before God…" and "the dead were judged out of those things which were written in the books, according to their works…" Only the wicked on the earth were killed, and become "dead," so it seems any righteous people are not included in this "second death" resurrection. My guess is, the righteous will remain in natural bodies for the new heaven and earth. It is only a guess, for John does not tell us. However, we must consider this:

> 15. And whosoever was not found written in the
> book of life was cast into the lake of fire. (King
> James Version, Revelation 20)

This verse at least hints that there might be people whose names *will be* in the Book of Life. John does not make it clear: are the living righteous at this time to receive resurrection bodies? John does not tell us.

The New Heaven and Earth

> 1. And I saw a new heaven and a new earth: for the first heaven and the first earth were passed away; and there was no more sea. (King James Version, Revelation 21)

After the old heaven and earth are gone, and after the White throne judgment, God will create a new heaven and earth—this new earth with have no sea. God then places the city of New Jerusalem down upon the new earth.

I would guess, at this time, we could say "and they lived happily ever after." John takes us on into eternity.

> 6. And he said unto me, It is done. I am Alpha and Omega, the beginning and *the end*. I will give unto him that is athirst of the fountain of the water of life freely. (King James Version, Revelation 21)

Printed in the United States
By Bookmasters